The Many Facets of A. Starr:

Purifying Truths

Authored by Amelia Isom

The Many Facets of A. Starr:

Purifying Truths

Copyright © 2019 by Amelia Isom

ISBN (978-164713-686-4)

Dedication

"The Many Facets of A. Starr: Purifying Truths," is dedicated to my children & women who inspired, guided, motivated, and made an eternal impression on me.

The truths disclosed within this memoir were revealed for the following purposes: Primarily, I needed my children to understand and know who I am, why I am the way that I am, how I *became* who I am today... and more importantly my constant evolution. Secondly, I finally understood the way I experienced and perceived my life is ultimately the truth. I cannot change it, I cannot hide from it, and essentially, I needed to be liberated from my life's ugliness, the confusion, the shame, and most of all the notion that I am a "one-dimensional being."

At this point in my life I realize that I am a multi-layered, multi-dimensional, multifaceted individual. So, if and when I seemingly don't make sense, I understand that the person I am, is on a constant journey of self-discovery. Therefore, there will always be multiple facets that define A. Starr.

Foreword

The life that we are born into is never chosen by us. However, it is destined for us… unsurprisingly, if some of us had our way we would map out our lives "perfectly," without hesitation. Our lives would be pain-free, worry-free, stress-free, and hardship or detriment would never cross our paths.

Fortunately, we cannot dictate our lives and the things that occur inevitably or unfortunately. Amelia's life, thus far, has been nothing less than a journey of determination, resilience, hope, and a bodacious will to become and be the undisputable embodiment of everything her past, circumstances, and experiences said she couldn't or wouldn't be.

Amelia allowed the hardships, unfortunate events, and unorthodox lessons to be the fuel that propelled her to this point in her life. Even though, the reality she was born into seemed destitute, perplexed, and some may even say damned…Amelia is A. Starr, she is a cosmic being of strength and fortitude. Truthfully, no one will ever touch a star, but we will always be able to see the beauty and light of A. Starr no matter what!

Grace & Peace,

Victoria Holmes
Literary Impressions LLC
Chief Editor & Literary Consultant

Table of Contents

Foreword iv

Introduction v

Chapters

1: Born into Brokenness 1

2: Mommy Dearest vs. Mommy Sincerest 32

3: Shake & Bake 50

4: I Didn't Choke on the Bones… 77

5: Mission Unaccomplished 87

6: I am My Mother's Child 91

7: Evolving Transitions 95

About the Author.. 103

Introduction

Life

Challenges

Crossroads, Choices, Changes

Accomplishments, Disappointments

Growth, Maturity

Legacy

As I reflect on the many paths that lead to who I am today and who I am becoming, I often wonder why I was born into a family of dysfunction? Or planted deeply in fertile soil where each obstacle I overcame was preparation for me to blossom and inspire those who encounter me?

I was not consulted as to where I wanted to be born or to whom. Honestly, I don't know if I would have made a better choice. I do not understand the intricate working and why things are the way they are. They just are. I have learned through life's experiences that with a combination of endurance and strength mixed with a little imagination, the journey of life is worthwhile. These vital elements contribute to my evolution.

Although, we cannot control the circumstances surrounding our birth; it is our perception that will either demolish or preserve us. These open confessions regarding my life reveal the irony of experiencing "the good and the bad" *simultaneously*. Some are dismal and showed where I was dragged through the briar patches of life… while other times I seemed to float carelessly like dandelion gliding in the wind. There is not an instruction manual for life, thus it is all trial and error, disaster and triumph, but more importantly personal evolution… we cannot evolve without going through "our" *processes*; the process (life) inevitably leads us to our liberation, *eventually*…

Flashback: Before I entered this world…

"Stop you are hurting me! I'm sorry, please stop!" Carol pleaded. "I'm sorry!" "Damn right you sorry," shouted a cold and raspy voice. Blood splattered from Carol's mouth as she was slapped so violently that she took flight colliding into the opposing wall. She sobbed quietly, in the fetal position.

Bill continued to shout, "You and that damn baby making me miss out on a lot of money. Shit no one wants a sick fat trick! I can't even give your sorry ass away now!" As he continuously kicked her in her side, while crying Carol cautiously uttered... "I only got a month and a few weeks left. I promise, I will make it up to you daddy. I will, I promise!" "Oh, *I know*, you got that shit right! You will definitely make it up! And if that lil' motherfucker a girl, she gonna work this shit off too! Now get up and go clean your sorry ass!"

Carol attempted to get up. However, she stumbled a few steps and then fell forward toward Bill. Instead of helping her, he backed away and watched her fall. When she hit the floor he yelled, "Trick get up!" Carol's bloody nose dripped down onto her lips, her vision was blurred in one eye and the other eye was swollen shut. She was mercilessly battered and weak. It was impossible for her to muster up the strength to stand even with help!

Bill realized Carol needed to go to hospital, and the thought of showing any remorse or concern for her angered him even more. So Bill lugged Carol into his car like a bag of trash, and spewed obscenities at her the entire 15 minute drive. "Trick stop bleeding all over my seats, I knew shoulda left you!"

When they arrived at the hospital, Bill didn't escort Carol inside. Instead with the same violent demeanor, he hatefully threw her out of his car! Carol stumbled inside trying not to fall, but her strength betrayed her. Her pregnant and battered body fell to the ground, while bystanders looked at her in shock and disgust… After what seemed like an unending couple of minutes, Carol was assisted by hospital staff and rushed to the maternity ward.

Why did I, an innocent child have to enter life through such a treacherous path, that seemingly led to a dead end… broke - IN - this… my life. WHY?

Chapter 1

"Born *into* Brokenness"

Family

From the beginning of her very essence, my mom's future had a bleak overcast. She was left in the hospital by her biological parents, who feared they would not be able to care for her properly. They were young and wanted the best for their precious little girl. They were barely able to make it financially trying to support themselves. Jobs were scarce and almost impossible to come by. They simply could not feed another mouth.

The unselfish decision to leave their daughter in the hospital gave her an opportunity to have a better life than what they could provide. The young couple despondently signed the necessary paperwork relinquishing their parental rights and responsibilities. With burdened hearts and tears streaming down their face, both parents kissed baby Carol one final time and hesitantly handed her to a social worker.

Carol was nurtured and cared for in the hospital for a few more days before being transported to an orphanage. She was a brown beauty with the cutest toothless smile and bright brown eyes full of promise. Shortly after turning three months old, she was placed in a loving foster home. Her foster parents were in their fifties, oh how they loved her so... but, Carol's upbringing was very different from other children.

Estelle, Big Momma, was a bright-skinned round woman, with thin dark wavy hair, which she kept pinned up in a bun. She wore only dresses and skirts due to her COGIC religious beliefs. Although, she was a housewife and an excellent cook, Big Momma was far from the traditional women of her time. She was not meek or weak, but rather a trailblazer of sorts. A concoction of sweet and sour, loving, strong willed, ambitious and stern woman. Family was her delight. She made certain that the quaint public housing they lived in was a home. It was always tidy and filled with the aroma of home cooking. Much of her time was spent volunteering at the church. She served on various boards helping wherever help was needed. With only an eighth-grade education, she was surprisingly knowledgeable on several topics. She had traveled the world visiting places like Quebec, Germany, Cuba and Africa! She could read and write, which was almost unheard of for a woman of color during her time. She seldom worked outside the home but did not hesitate to do so in order to provide for her family.

Samuel, Big Daddy, was a medium built tall man with a complexion so dark and smooth it almost looked like silky soot. This undisputed brave man was nothing less than a hero. He was a reserved but friendly army veteran who served in World War II and took great pride in caring for his family. Big Daddy's large statue camouflaged his teddy bear persona. He was optimistic and kind, easy to talk to and never judgmental. It was as if he had the privilege of seeing life through a different lens than the rest of the world. Big Daddy rolled with each punch life gave him and he never complained.

Brinda, a beautiful mocha colored 2-year-old toddler, was adopted into the family a year earlier. Brinda had beautiful long tresses that graced her shoulders. From their very first interaction, Carol and Brinda established an immediate bond. Brinda's sheepish smile welcomed Carol as she handed her a doll baby and pulled her towards her playroom. A sisterhood was born that would endure a lifetime. These girls had conquests, of triumphs and defeats that they conquered together.

Granny Annie had thick, soft, dark gray, wavy hair framing her wrinkle-free caramel colored face. Though she was wheelchair bound, she was certainly not dependent on anyone. She serenaded neighbors and bystanders with her angelic voice humming ole' Negro spirituals as she sat by the window watching people in the park below. She was constantly complimenting and encouraging everybody who she encountered. Grannie generously greeted everyone with her toothless smile while sharing the songs in her heart. She was a woman of wisdom, having been through and seen things many only heard about.

She was a daughter of the "Masser." Yes, her Negro mom was raped by their Masser on a Virginia Plantation. She was told that her "daddy" was an arrogant and demanding man who always got his way! Granny professed she does not remember him.

When she was only a toddler, approximately three years old, that her mother was given her *"freedom papers!"* The war was over, and just like that she was free. Granny was too young to be considered a slave, so her mother's papers made her free. Masser gave them thirty acres of farmland, I guess this helped him clear his conscience and reconcile or justify rapping Granny's mom and compensate for expenses that come with rearing a child. He then sold the remainder of the land and moved, and they never saw or heard from him again.

Granny told several stories; she was a living-breathing history book! Her round, now dim, eyes had witnessed the end of slavery, horse-drawn buggies to model Ts, railroads being built and subways. She lived through segregation, the civil rights movement, and several historical marches and protest. Yes, she'd experienced all of it and had a story about each life-changing event.

Addition to the Family

When Carol was in the sixth grade, Richard, an eight-month-old bundle of joy became part of the family. Big Daddy had always wanted a boy. Richard was vibrant and happy all the time. He was the cure Carol needed. He was not adopted either. She *finally* had someone she could relate to and connect with. Carol and Brinda took pride in helping Big Momma take care of Richard. Unfortunately, after a few short weeks the family learned that Richard had a blood condition that made him extremely ill, sometimes he had to be hospitalized. He was easily tired and unable to play for long periods of time. Lil' Richard bruised easily and always seemly had something in his throat causing him to constantly clear his throat or cough. Each family member carefully snuggled with Richard, or "Richie as Granny called him.

He got special treatment because he was the only boy

and the youngest. He used it to his advantage when

trying to get something or do something he knew he

shouldn't. Richie was a little stinker; he enjoyed each day

of his short-lived life.

Every day he gave love and felt it in return. At the

age of three, Richard was diagnosed with leukemia. My

mom (Carol) needed his existence because he affirmed

hers'. When Richie was at home Carol was very attentive

to his needs. She nurtured him as if he was her very own

son. He was spoiled by everyone in the family. Year after

year he triumphed over health obstacles and became and

encouragement to both Carol and Brinda.

In comparison, Carol was nurtured and cared for

as if she was Big Momma's and Big Daddy's very own

biological daughter. She was a very happy go lucky child

that was full of gratitude. She enjoyed the things that most people simply overlooked. Carol had a very light and carefree spirit. She enjoyed playing with her sister and brother.

One day, as she played on the swing during recess, a girl started laughing at Carol. Some other children joined the mockery and started teasing her by calling her names like ugly and bald headed. Carol ignored them and continued to swing. Then the little bullies pushed her so high she thought she was going to fall. The swing started to buckle. Afraid that she'd be thrown from the swing, she jumped and scuffed her knees. The pain inside was enough to make her cry, but she adamantly fought to restrain every tear. She would not dare allow *them* to see her cry. After she dusted herself off, she ran to the group to confront the girl that pushed her. As she approached them, they laughed and yelled, "You're just a stupid foster kid that nobody wants because you're too ugly!" Carol's fury exploded with each punch, but she wondered if their words were true. POW, a punch to the bully's stomach! A foster kid? Splat, a slap across the bully's face! What is a foster kid, is that when nobody wants you?

"Carol! Carol! Stop it right now!" Yelled Mrs. Wright as she attempted to pull her off the instigator. Both girls were called into the office and suspended for the rest of the day. When Big Momma came to get Carol, she checked-out Brinda too. As they rode the subway home, Carol questioned why her name was different, and why she was a foster child. Big Momma passionately clarified that she had *chosen* each of them, even Carol. She explained that she loved her equally as much as she did Brinda. She sadly confessed that she was not sure that she could afford another child but knew she could love another one. That was the only reason why she *chose* to foster Carol.

Carol was ultimately devastated. Suddenly, her perfect world was shattered as she realized she was "not really one of the family." She tried to digest the news she'd just learned, but it was hard for her elementary mind to understand. Brinda encouraged her that no matter what they would always be sisters. No matter the last name or where they were.

Big Momma was from a large family and had several brothers and one sister. She often gave examples of how blood family can be mean and uncaring, attempting to prove to Carol that being blood-related was not more important than being "love related". As Carol grew older, she struggled with self-worth. She often felt less than others because she didn't know her biological family. She started to harbor resentment and anger. As it festered, she hated the reality and uncertainty of being a "foster child." She started observing others with similar physical features and wondered if they were her biological cousins? If they were her brothers, or sisters even? She pondered this daily, to the point of obsession… she wanted to know who she was and why had she been dealt this hand?

This victim mentality lead to depression. She began to rebel at school and at home. Carol got into several fights and became verbally aggressive at home. Inevitably, this led to school detentions and suspensions. At home Brinda always quickly defended Carol and attempted to keep her from being punished.

Big Momma's consequences were often minuscule, as she tried to convince Carol that family is so much more than simply a blood line. She tried to persuade Carol that she was loved just as much as

Brinda. Carol believed this at times and at other times she did not. She felt as if a cloud hung over her, sometimes the sunshine peeked through and on other days the overcast lingered unapologetically.

One day the girls came home from school to find Big Momma sobbing quietly in Big Daddy's arms. Although, it was a sunny afternoon, the curtains were closed, the apartment was dimly lit and had a melancholy atmosphere. This was very odd because Big Momma always opened the curtains to let the sunshine in.

Brinda and Carol had never seen Big Momma so distraught. Her hair was scruffy, and her makeup smudged. Big Daddy's face was somber and stone-like… his eyes were bloodshot red. He sat stoically, his arms wrapped tightly around Big Momma, while he slowly swayed back and forth and hummed a soft soothing melody in Big Momma's ear.

"What's wrong," the girls inquired anxiously.

"Richard! Richard! Richard," screamed Big Momma!

What about Richard? The girls asked as they ran to

Richard's room. "Riiiiichaaaarddddd!" sobbed Big

Momma

Granny Annie came out of the family room and

took Carol and Brinda to her room. Then she attempted

to explain the occurrence of death, life and eternal life.

She told them everybody has an expiration date. Finally,

to comfort them she quoted a scripture, "to be absent

from the body, is to be present with the Lord." She said,

"Richie no longer has to suffer, he is in heaven now!"

Granny's heart was heavy with hurt, but she tried

to find comfort Carol and Brinda with her words.

"Although Richie ain't with us, he always be watchin'

ov'r us." The girls whaled inconsolably. Why Richard?

He was so young. What type of God would snatch my

brother away like that? "He didn't even get to go to school!" Carol bawled uncontrollably; she was grief-stricken.

In middle school, the girls were "allowed" to join the girl scouts. Big Momma loved the idea of females courageously bonding together and becoming confident leaders. The motto was right up her alley… to Serve God (She always did something with one of the committees at church) and my country (Big Daddy was a soldier in WWII), and to help people at all times (Big Momma had a heart for missions).

Carol loved the girl scouts and earning badges. She made friends and learned to trust others through teamwork. Carol proudly participated in community events, she served the elderly, and improved the environment by planting trees, and picked up trash on adopted highways.

As a teenager, Carol constantly "tested the limits." She met some friends in girl scouts who she became close with. They went to separate schools and only saw each other during Girl Scout meetings. They always had "extra" adventures on their camping excursions.

One scorching summer night, the girls waited until the scout leaders were asleep. Then they tiptoed out of the camp area, climbed the metal fence that surrounded the pool, and jumped in to take a swim. Initially, it was like any other secret escapade. They had fun splashing and floating. Soon they started playing "Marco Polo."

Carol was a very strong swimmer, but Michelle and Rachel not so much. The girls were having so much fun they *almost* forgot that they had snuck in… they frolicked in pool with tightly closed eyes yelling

"Marco... Polo ...Marco!" It wasn't long before they noticed they were now in the deep end of the pool.

Michelle and Rachel began to panic. Carol tried to take control of the situation and calm them down. Rachel grabbed onto to Carol and would not let her go. Carol struggled to swim and pulling her to shallow end of pool so she could get out.

Immediately, Carol swam back for Michelle. She had just been wailing and screaming, but now it was eerily quiet. Carol saw Rachel running down the side of the pool with tears in her eyes, she was helpless and could only watch as Carol swam frantically to save Michelle who wasn't screaming anymore.

Actually, she wasn't even moving. Michelle was floating face-down in the pool! Carol struggled desperately to get Michelle to the edge of the pool, where Rachael helped her pull Michelle's lifeless body out of the water.

Rachael and Carol were traumatized! What could they do? Who could help? Should they leave her? Should they split up and run? They decided to stay together and climbed back over the fence and went back to the campground for help.

The Girl Scout leaders called for help and ran to the pool, unlocked the gate and began CPR on Michelle. The sound of each compression pierced Carol's ears as she watched hoping for recovery, knowing that she'd never see Michelle alive again.

As she was led away from the scene, the rustic cracking of her friend's ribs breaking, in an attempt to revive her... terrified Carol. The image and sound stayed in her mind for years to come. The guilt, the grief, the pain was unbearably heart-wrenching. Why did they have to go out that night? Why couldn't she save both of her friends? Why was this night so different?

These young girls just wanted to have some fun, as they mischievously did what they had done so many times before. However, this time their frolicking led to a tragic fatality.

After this incident, Carol began to have visions and dreams frequently. She often kept them to herself because when she confessed them, she was placed in therapy and evaluated mentally. Carol endured several exploratory and intrusive mental evaluations including painful brain stimulation via electric shock. Since she was a foster kid, the case workers had the final say on her medical and mental health care. The state was more than receptive to any and all diagnoses and treatments the doctors proposed for foster kids. This financially benefited several agencies with more federal funding monies.

Occasionally, Carol secretly shared her dreams with Brinda. One of her dreams was so realistic, she was compelled to share it with Brinda and even with Big Momma. Carol dreamed that one morning Granny Annie rolled herself into the kitchen and just kept rolling. She rolled herself right through the kitchen window. It was almost as if she was floating in the air over the park below and then she just disappeared!

Big Momma was a spiritual person and had been visited by her deceased sister. Before she was married, during the great depression, she was a live-in housekeeper/nanny. She recalled laying in her bed, about to go to sleep when a bright light appeared. Big Momma was so afraid she stayed still and just stared at the light. As the light got closer, it became clearer and she was not afraid at all as she realized it was her sister… her deceased sister staring back with a peaceful, admirable look on her face. Big Momma set up to focus and poof she was gone!

Big Momma had no verbal response to Carol's vision this time, a somber mood overcame her. She began to prepare herself mentally as if she knew this was a sign, a warning of sorts... she was going to lose her mother *soon*. A few months later, Granny Annie rolled herself into the kitchen like she did every morning.

While the girls were at the table waiting for Big Momma to serve breakfast, Granny Annie sat at the table by the kitchen window eerily gazing out at the park below with a glassy stare. She began to tremble and shake faster and faster like a phone on vibrate.

When she stopped shaking Big Momma walked over to the window and slowly opened it. She believed that this set Granny's spirit free. Just like that, Granny was gone.

Carol was in awe as she remembered her dream and how Granny explained death to her when Richard died. There was a surreal peace in the house as they all came to grips with Granny's eternal transition. They were able to find comfort in the scripture she recited so many times, "to be absent from the body is to be present with the Lord."

Carol completed middle school and looked forward to joining her sister in high school. However, when Brinda was in 10th grade, Big Momma decided she was getting boy crazy. With Big Momma, reality was skewed. She assumed and it was so...period! No facts needed. She never talked to them about sex, or dating, or female personal development or even hygiene for that matter! She just made her assumptions based on God knows what and acted on them. So, it was no need in trying to correct, rectify, or justify it.

And just like that, the state of Virginia became Brinda's new home. She was sent to stay with family and finish High School. First Richard! Then Granny! Now Brinda… Carol was devastated. She felt all alone and believed she was on borrowed time too. What would she do when her time ran out?

She was afraid of the uncertainty regarding her future. Carol, often worried that she would be sent to another torturous foster home! She just could not let that happen. It was this fear and her life's previous traumas that caused her to seek desperately for a place of belonging, a place of love, a place of security. She was mentally exhausted, and she begin to do poorly in school. She became withdrawn and careless at home. Eventually she dropped out of school. Life viciously catapulted Carol into a whirlwind of thoughtless living where she accepted rejection and desolate hopelessness as her reality.

One day, Carol was at the park swinging and collecting her thoughts, a handsome, well-dressed man introduced himself and initiated a conversation. Carol was flabbergasted that this man was interested in talking to her. He gave flattering compliments and offered to take her to lunch. Carol loved the attention. She knew she should not get in the car with *that* strange man, but she took the risk and they went to a local diner.

As they walked in heads turned, she felt like a star! Bill asked her to spend the night with him. She was so young, naive, and innocent that she willingly went to Bills place. When they arrived, there were other older women there. Bill introduced her to them and escorted her to his room. "Who were all these women and why were they all here" Carol wondered.

It seemed a little off, but she didn't dare ask any questions, she longed to spend more time with Bill and loved the attention he gave her. That night, Bill told her how much he loved her as he lustfully groped her trembling body. The words were sweet, but Carol was afraid. She had never kissed a boy before. She was unsure what was next but afraid to disappoint *him*.

Then Bill tied a belt around her tiny arm until a vein popped up as if it was crying for mercy. Every move Bill made was evil and calculated, as he injected a clear liquid into her vein. He removed the belt and whispered in Carol's ear, "Just relaxxx..." A warming sensation spread through her body, everything appeared hazy, nothing hurt mentally or physically *anymore*. It was a feeling she'd never felt before. Bill caressed her and penetrated seventeen-year-old Carol's body – physically, mentally, emotionally, and fatefully.

The next morning, he woke her up by kissing her stating, "You a woman now, you my woman. Last night was euphoric. You were the best I ever had; you are definitely *good enough* to keep all to myself." Not knowing what Bill meant by this and still a bit groggy Carol smiled and went back to sleep. When she woke, Bill took her shopping and on a dinner date. Carol was blindly happy. Bill had Carol go on dates with a few of his male friends. She hated the sex but loved the rewards. The feeling of being loved and cared about. The nice clothes and all the attention. The high of heroin kept her from thinking too much about the sex. She just did what she was told, when she was told, how she was told. The overnight escapade turned into weeks. Carol was not allowed to call Big Momma or Big Daddy although she'd asked numerous times. She wanted to let them know she was okay and was being taken care of by a really *nice* man.

Bill promised her he'd meet them when he took her home. Bill never left her side. It was no longer flattering, it was suffocating. As quick a Carol fell in love, she also fell out of it… now she felt trapped. What had she gotten herself into?

She pleaded with Bill to take her home so he did, but he was too busy to meet her family. However, he promised to come back and pick her up. Carol was welcomed with open arms by Big Daddy, who was having a smoke on the balcony when she arrived. When Big Momma came from her church meeting, she was happy to see Carol as well. She noticed something was different, she just couldn't put her finger on it.

Carol stayed and told of her dreamy husband to be. She promised she'd bring him by one day. Day after day Carol expected Bill to return but he did not. She realized she was pregnant and was anxious to share the 'good' news with Bill! They were going to be a family...

Carol kept her secret as she wanted Bill to be the first to know. When she could no longer wait, she took the subway over to his place to tell him the news, she had missed her period and thought she was pregnant. Bill was different when she arrived, not very welcoming. He seemed to be annoyed.

Carol thought she could cheer him up, with the 'good' news. She gave him a passionate kiss and sprung the news on him. It ignited his fury and not his delight! She was devastated! Bill let her know he didn't want no babies! Carol stayed there with Bill, hoping that he'd change his mind. Bill continued to use heroin more frequently more. He became more distant towards Carol.

The compliments stopped. Eventually, like the other women she found herself on the corner satisfying Johns.

Carol played the hand she was dealt. Her thought of freedom was achieved with Bill, but her pregnancy revealed what she thought *was* love.

If Carol (Mom) could tell her story…

My mother deserted me when I was born. I went from house to house as I grew up. It was as if no one wanted me. In every foster home that I was placed in except for Big Momma's, the families were abusive verbally, physically, or sexually. As I look back over the numerous homes, the Johnston's home was the worst. It was a Thursday in June 1963. I was sixteen years old. My foster family was going on vacation to see Brinda.

They were forced to place me in respite care until their return because the social workers would not let me cross state lines. Respite care was temporary placement where families could put their foster children until they returned from vacations and such. I was to be at the Johnston's home for seven days, until the following Thursday.

I had a reputation for running away. That night Mr. Johnston begin threatening and swearing at me and he told me, I better not even think of leaving his house until he said so. Mrs. Johnston, a small framed quiet woman, showed me to my room. The walls were a pale, dusty pink and the windows had prison-like iron bars on them. There was one small lamp in the corner, which gave off a dim smoky light.

Not long after we were in the room Mr. Johnston came in. He put handcuffs around my wrist and cuffed me to a chain, which was attached to the bedpost. Mrs. Johnston quietly tried soothing me, while telling me it was for my own good and not to fight back. My feet were then shackled together by Mr. Johnston, making it difficult to walk, and impossible to run. The chains were lightweight and allowed me to reach the corner of the room where a bedpan was placed, in case I needed to use the bathroom. I felt like

30

I was less than an animal. I had never been chained up and treated like a dog before. I vowed to myself, I would never give anyone the opportunity to treat me this way again.

Thursday did not come fast enough but it finally arrived. I was unleashed and dolled up just in time to meet with the caseworker that was to take me back to my foster family. This was it. This was my chance to be free. As the caseworker packed my possessions, I was instructed to wait in the car. Instead, I hid under the car parked next to the caseworker's car. She called me a few times. After no response she left, saying Carol is on the run again. This run was not like the rest. I did not want to be found and placed in another home. They were all horrible. I needed to be free.

Chapter 2

Mommy Dearest vs. Mommy Sincerest

There are certain things I just couldn't do, I mean after all I was a princess, royalty, I was taught to never sit with my legs gaped open. I sat-up straight and was beautifully postured. I had a 'perfect' chocolate complexion therefore, playing outside and "unintentionally" tanning my skin was forbidden.

Precious me, I had to play in the shade or stay in the house. While at school I had a blast as I played on the playground with my classmates… the worry of sun-tanning was the furthest thing from my mind, "I was having fun!" As soon as I walked through the doors of Big Momma's home, she scolded me, "You were on the playground *again*!" Immediately she slapped Noxzema all over my face, I loved the cooling sensation, but I hated the fact that she did not want me to get "darker."

Unsurprisingly, my complexion was the same shade of chocolate before and after the Noxzema [but Big Momma just knew, her "home remedy" was undoing my "sun-damage"]. I didn't see anything wrong with the dark skin, after all she was in love with Big Daddy despite his dark skin. He was the darkest person I'd ever seen! Big Momma said girls are different, they shouldn't be so dark. I had to keep my beautiful complexion 'perfect,' so a nice man would marry me. At that moment, I decided I was gonna be as dark as I possibly could get... when I became 'older,' I was gonna play outside in the sun *and* tan on the beach too! Just wait, I'm gonna be dark *and still be beautiful!*

At two years old Carol sent me to Virginia to live with Big Momma and Big Daddy, in the country... they had a small quaint home; with two bedrooms on one acre of land. There a garden behind our house, and in the middle of it there was a beautiful weeping Willow tree. This was the tree that caused me to weep on many occasions, as it was from this tree, I had to pick my own switch to get 'a whoopin' whenever Big Momma decided I needed "the rod of correction."

We had our pump-house and we had a shed...So the pump house was a small house the size of an extra small closet. It housed the well, and it was covered with a heavy top. There was a pump in the house and a spigot. There was very little room in it for anything else inside it.

During the summer months, at sunrise Big Momma and I worked in the garden. Once Big Daddy got up, she made him breakfast. Big Momma groomed me for marriage to a nice man... so, learning to cook and clean was essential.

I wasn't allowed to listen to "worley-music" [aka secular]. I wasn't allowed to wear mini-skirts, red lipstick, and even perfume was prohibited. *"Mini-skirts, you are dressed like a whore, red lipstick you look like a whore, and wearing that perfume makes you smell like a whore..."* I can clearly hear Big Momma's voice.

On any given day in the spring [whether I had school or not], my grandmother and I woke up right at sunrise and went into the garden and proceeded with the grueling task of planting seeds, watering the garden, tilling the garden, *and* harvesting the garden... I was in the first grade! This was not my idea of "fun."

At the peak of the spring's disrespectful sunlight... we took a break to make breakfast for Big Daddy, which I could never eat... Big Daddy ate scrambled eggs. My mouth would water as these fluffy morsels were cooked. I was a lady, never to eat eggs, unless cooked in a food like cake cornbread, etc. A plain egg was not for ladies as the white squiggly pieces are "sperm!" Big Momma explained with the most disgusting look on her face. "Ladies don't swallow sperm," I was taught. Hmmmm, I wondered why. Where does sperm come from, wait exactly what is this sperm you speak of...Clueless, but I certainly did not eat eggs.

On school days I usually completed my morning chores prior to catching the bus. We only had two schools, Surry Elementary and Surry High. Everyone rode the same bus. Elementary students sat at the front and high school students sat in the back. The schools were across the street from each other.

I grew up in a small country town… we lived in a small ranch house and enjoyed the simple pleasures of life. We didn't have much, but I thought we were Surry's very own "Jefferson's…" *I should have known we weren't rich, as we waited in a line for government cheese along with all the other "rich people."*

God's grace allowed my grandmother to perform the miracle of caring for me every day while maintaining her day-to-day life. I was often told "no," so I wouldn't expect things... but somehow Big Momma always bought me what I wanted *when* she could afford it. I wasn't allowed to get a job, one of Big Momma's many mantras was "you have the rest of your life to work, there's a lot of things going on out there besides getting money... and you won't be a part of it!" My grandmother treated me as if I was my Mom.

Consequently, this was her way of protecting and preventing me from "being like my Mom." She thought that somehow, I was gonna get pregnant and that was the furthest thing from my mind. I didn't even know how to get pregnant! During my childhood and adolescent years, I wasn't allowed to go and do the things that my peers were able to do. I thought it was mean at the time but in retrospect, I appreciate it...*it* molded me into the woman I am today.

Childhood

Big Momma took me to live with her shortly after I was potty-trained. She was elated to have me... she treated me as if I was a precious commodity. I was her redemption… another chance for her to prove to herself that she had not failed as a mother. I *loved* Big Daddy; he was a quiet man. He just let me do whatever I wanted. We had tickle fest and secretly watched late-night TV. He even allowed me to jump on his bed. In his eyes, I was perfect. I made him laugh and forget about his kidney problems. I was Big Daddy's therapy and he was my hero.

My cousins came over and spent the weekend sometimes. It was at this time that I felt extra special! I'd wake up earlier than them and Big Momma would already be awake. She'd give me a slice of pound cake with hot tea, before we headed out to the garden. When we had dinner, she always picked the bones out my fish, while they were left to pick their own bones out. She didn't want me to choke.

Big Momma was a firm believer of not going to bed hungry, so if I didn't like what she cooked... I could always have whatever I *wanted*, because I was her prized possession! *They* had to eat what was cooked or be hungry. No, this double standard was not fair, but I took full advantage of these minor perks.

On the other hand, my life was very structured. I was only allowed to watch a 1/2 hour of TV on school nights and an hour of TV whenever there was no school.

I was outside quite a bit exploring and pretending... I was quite imaginative. Big Momma had a subscription to Ebony magazine. I used to cut the people out and pack them up in my bike mobile and drive off.

We had several trees in our yard. Each tree was one of my imaginary friend's house, and I'd stop by and visited each of them. Sometimes we made mud pies, other times we'd go on escapades that ended at the rainbow.

One year, I was allowed to plant my own garden. It had popcorn, grey trouser beans, sweet peas, lima beans, and watermelon. We grew strawberries and mint in front of the house... the fragrance welcomed everyone who visited.

In Surry, community was the main means of survival. We all helped each other out often using the trading and bartering system. Some families herded cows, some people had chickens, and others had pigs. After the butcher cut up the slaughtered animal then it was distributed among the community. Those who had crops, shared when they were harvested. We seldom went to the store to purchase anything, because we had everything.

The women in the community made the butter, sausages, preserved the fruit and vegetables. I remember watching, as a little girl, sausage be ground and stuffed into chitlins. I loved the smell of the smokehouse where the ham and bacon were cured. We had large barrel sized tins which kept our flour and meal. There was always more than enough. We blanched our vegetables and froze them fresh ourselves. We pickled tomatoes, cucumbers and watermelon rinds. We canned tomatoes, jams and preserves. Life was good... simple but good!

Adolescent Years:

In 8th grade, we transitioned to the high school. My eighth-grade class were the first 8th graders to be in the high school! The class of '92 proudly took our place as Thatimore's in the high school building. It was in 10th grade when my ego exploded, my attitude worsened, and I begin to struggle with academics. I stopped applying myself and I failed.

It seemed like everyone was into name brand clothes and I was teased unmercifully because I didn't have the latest and the greatest. I became a fighter. I verbally attacked anyone who dared to cross me... and if that led to a physical altercation I didn't back down.

I knew words hurt because they hurt me! I made sure that others felt my wrath. It didn't matter to me child or adult; I spoke my mind and explicitly expressed my anger.

Naturally, I was at the age where boys were no longer "yucky" or disgusting, but a favorable option. "Yummy…" [I finally ate the eggs]. Inevitably, I was a little flirtatious. Back at home my grandmother seemed to have been dreading this stage of my life. I had begun my menstrual cycle, and when I did… Big Momma just didn't understand why my cramps were horrendous. It was the worst pain I'd ever experienced. I stayed in the nurse's office… nausea and the excruciating cramps kept me in a fetal position. Every single month it was torture… and to add injury to insult, my grandmother accused me of getting pregnant and having a coat hanger abortion! Frequently, she berated me, and told me "Stop, all that putting on. It's impossible for anybody to hurt that bad!"

Ridiculous as it was, I didn't have personal access to feminine hygiene products … Big Momma issued them out to me. Without fail, she antagonized me about my need of so many sanitary products. She accused me of "faking it" yelling, "You're not even bleeding, this is ketchup!"

The accusations lead to arguments and finally I had had it. I was humiliated enough and would prove to her I was on my period!

As she sat on the bedside accusing me, I bent over naked from the waist down and showed her! Yes, I showed her no ketchup, no pregnancy, and then demanded my pad. She gave it to me. I continued to carry on yelling how I told her I wasn't pregnant. I stormed out the house to catch the school bus. I was livid! I didn't even know how to get pregnant; I was a virgin and had never even kissed a boy!

When I came home from school that day all of my things were packed in a van. My grandmother stood at the door, waving. The flap of skin under her arm moved slowly back-and-forth [an image that will forever be etched in my mind]. I was not allowed to go back in her home, the van drove me away… I was numb, I finally understood a portion of my mother's pain. No goodbyes, no understanding, and just like that no more "grandma's favorite." Devastation and betrayal consumed me… reality cold-cocked me and left me speechless. What had I done so terrible to be snatched away from the life I knew, the life I wanted, the life I believed I needed?

So, there I was, scared senseless... I could not believe Big Momma had put me out for nothing. She accused be of being pregnant so much she actually believed it!

As I rode with the social worker, seemingly I felt every bump in the road. Although, it was only a 10-15-

minute ride it felt like hours! Where could I go? What could I do…? I was only fifteen years old. My whole world changed instantly; I had no control!

Being a sarcastic teenager, when questioned about my mother I lied and retorted, "I don't know, I ain't got no Mom," "She is in jail!" I said whatever my mind thought to get "them" off my back. Another cousin allowed me to stay with her and her family. It was perfect. I immediately blended in with her children.

She and her husband treated me like one of their own children. This bliss was short lived, after one week, not only did they find my mom… they were already processing the arrangements for me to live with her.

One day, I was called to the front office while at school… lo and behold, there *she* was…. standing with open arms. I was very happy to see her; my Mom was like a rare treat that I only received on special occasions.

At the same time, I was devastated! Totally shocked, when I found out I had to leave with her, that she was there to take me to Pennsylvania with her. My body crumpled to the floor in disbelief, I cried and begged her to at least let me say bye to my friends. She allowed me to return to class and waited until the end of the school day so I could say goodbye to my friends.

Ironically just like at Big Momma's *that day*, once again feelings of uncertainty regarding my future haunted me... Mom didn't drive, after all in the city there was no need for a driver's license. She had access to buses, cabs, and trains. We had to journey to Pennsylvania on the Greyhound bus. The long ride allowed us to catch up, reunite, and get to know each other.

Mom lightened my mood and filled the dreaded move with inspiration and hope. I wondered how far *I could go?* A new school, new life, and new adventures. In a matter of twenty-four hours my princess mentality was converted… I grew up instantly!

Once off the bus in Pennsylvania, I had an immediate reality check... I wasn't dreaming. No yelling for a cab for us, it was too expensive. We had to use our "chev-o-legs!" What was going on? Are we poor too!?! Since when did 'princesses' walk such long distances? And why was my Mom seemingly so happy about *this*?

Teenagers & Mothers

Okay, so here I am Princess Amelia… in the middle of Hallmanor [the south side projects], row 18 to be exact! I thought to myself "Well I guess this is what the rappers meant by *Thug Life*… the struggle was real and oh *so different*. Remember, I was "rich" and Big Momma's little trophy. *I was not in Kansas anymore*… it was a different world… my naivety made me ask questions. My curiosity was peaked!

What is that white powder? What is the liquid-stuff in the metal spoon? Oh my gosh, it was just like a movie! Am I in a New Jack City, *for real*? I could not move past that moment... my surroundings fascinated me. The blatant [but supposedly subliminal] drug transactions. People getting high and drunk, and stealing was a normal everyday thing! From the palace to the pit... this was an eye-opening experience for me. I started admiring the dope boys, I wanted the bamboo earrings, and all the other things we couldn't afford. I should have been afraid and leery of the 'fast-life...' Surprisingly, I was not, because I knew I was smarter than *them*. My "naïve" involvement was a means to an end... not a lifestyle I would live forever.

Chapter 3

Shake and Bake

There were several people that impacted and somewhat molded me into the person I *needed/wanted* to be while living in Hallmanor Projects. It was quite liberating "to be me!" My life was a myriad of ironic realities… some may have said "I was a good girl gone bad…" but this assumption could not be made about me because "they" didn't know me. I was "Shake," but I was unshakable and, on a mission, *to get back to Surry.*

My relationship began developing between my brother, sister and I, now that we resided in the same city. As our relationship grew, I visited them as often as I could. My brother, the youngest sibling resided with an Aunt, and my sister, the middle sibling lived with their grandmother. I was so excited to have *my* sister and felt obligated to take care of her when she visited me in the projects making sure no one "messed" with her.

Chuck, our stepdad took care of us. He worked at Burger King. He'd "drive" his bike with a generated light and rear-view mirrors to and from work. He often brought me home the leftovers Whoppers and frozen fries. There were many days that I had nothing but snacks and leftover Burger King for dinner. From the outside looking in, most would have assumed "I was living a *good* life, I wore the latest fashions, and kept a "hairdo," my nails stayed manicured, and my makeup kept me looking "purposely tanned."

Eric, was who I called my Big Brother and, in many ways, was my angel in disguise… sometimes an angel of light and other times an angel of darkness. Nonetheless I believe he was divinely put in my path. He was extremely smart, almost a genius... but he *chose* the street-life.

Life in the projects... major eye-opener, I grew up quickly! I lived life to the fullest. I made the most out of what I had and seized everyday as an opportunity to do better and get out of the generational death trap, Hallmanor. I became street-smart, but I knew I would not become enslaved to the lifestyle of the streets! I did what I had to do, to get what I needed... you know "the house, husband, two kids and a dog" type of life. Big Momma's words constantly echoed in my mind.

Early one morning there was a loud bang and a bunch of screams. Like always, I peeked out the window and noticed a shadowy figure by the mailbox in front of our house. It staggered away from the sidewalk and fell about five steps from my doorstep. Then there were sirens, and the crowd scattered, only a few people remained by his side. Once the sun rose, the neighborhood awakened, and came outside... I found out my classmate had been shot directly in front of my house! And he died!

In this eerie moment, I realized my mom and I shared the same gift. That week I kept having a recurring dream "about teeth..." until the night of the murder. I did not dream the night of the homicide. I had told mutual friends of my deceased classmate, *"Somebody is going to die."*

Ironically, the people I confessed this ill-fated dream to *knew* him. A friend reminded me stating, "Remember you said... you said... somebody was going to die." I felt perplexed as I thought about it. What was going on? When did I start this *again*? I was so afraid, I didn't care to know this type of information, and how fair was it that I knew of someone's demise, but they were faceless.

I didn't even get a chance to say good-bye. *This was a gift*...hmmmm not funny God, not funny at all. This was a gift that I wanted to return... don't keep giving *it* to me! I was angry, confused, and scared. Every day as I left my home, there it was the amorphous and eternally stained evidence of my former classmate's death. It was a grim reminder that life is short. *"Gone too soon"* was a horrid and humbling reality. Life is not *always* kind or fair, but its experiences are often unavoidable.

Mom and I used to play like sisters, I saw her as my best friend. I didn't keep secrets from her. I told her everything, from the day I skipped school and lost my virginity... to who shoplifted at the mall. There were no questions I didn't ask. I wanted to know everything like... "Ma, how big should a penis be?" "Why do people only "do it" at night? "Were you ever a stripper…?" We talked about so many things, I was very comfortable with Mom and trusted her knowledge. We dressed alike, drank together, we hung out *like we were best friends.* She was fun and loved to laugh. However, I had no idea she was an addict…

Whenever I wanted something, she got it, when she got her welfare check I got my portion of the money. Seems more than fair to me, she even gave me my portion of the food stamps. Life was good, I'd often walked up to Paxton Street to buy a box of steak from Murray's, as I always had a desire for the "finer things."

One horrid day, my world came crashing down, *again*! I came home from school and rushed upstairs to go to the bathroom like I did almost every day but this day there were two bags of white stuff in a gallon sized plastic bag on the bathroom floor. As an ignorant and former resident of Surry, I thought mom had been to the farmers market and bought some real flour... and like me had to rush to the bathroom to avoid an accident. Consequently, I believed she had forgotten the flour on the bathroom floor.

So, after I used the facilities, I waltzed downstairs with "the flour" and asked mom where to put it. She scoffed, "Give it to me!" I insisted that I should put it up. She was very adamant that I give it to her, because I was naive and in a playful mood, I refused.

This pissed mom off, but it was hilarious to me. I didn't understand why it was a big deal. As she tried to snatch it, I ducked and I ran, she followed me in pursuit of "the flour." I ran outside, and she was on my heels. I ran around the entire row of projects... mom desperately chased me! As I ran, the bag burst, and the flour spilled. "Oh well, dust storm..." I thought playfully tossing it in the air. Mom was 38 HOTTTT!!!! I couldn't understand why, over some damn flour of all things! Hell, after all we had more food stamps! What was the big deal?

This was the beginning of a very rocky relationship between me and Mom. But Why? It wasn't flour? What did Mom mean? It was cocaine? The drug, I, Princess Amelia *had touched drugs*! I just knew I was going to die. Why were drugs in my bathroom? What exactly was going on? I needed answers!

Oh yeah… it wasn't even my mom's cocaine! She worked for a dealer, mom cooked it, bagged it, and then she received a portion of it as payment for her work. I had caused guaranteed trouble for quite a few people... Oops, my bad!

I don't know how that situation was dealt with, but Chuck stepped in and saved the day. He always did. The young thugs respected him, as he had acquired OG status. Nobody made trouble with "Crazy one-armed Chuckie!"

Mom became more and more distant with me. I grieved for our relationship. Shortly after this incident, my sister and brothers' grandmother died. Since she was *my* sister, I wanted her to stay with me. I persuaded her to come stay with us in the projects. She eagerly accepted as she wanted to spend more time with me too.

I now looked at Mom differently. I couldn't believe she actually did drugs. How disgusting! I went from looking up to her to looking down on her. I was unforgivingly critical, unmercifully judgmental, and I had lost all respect for her.

Yet, I loved her dearly and longed for her to get off drugs and be my best friend *again*. I begged and pleaded with my Mom to go to a drug rehab and get clean. She'd go, stay for a few days and then she'd leave and immediately return to the streets *again*. Mom came up with the outrageous stories to tell me after rehab. I wanted to trust that she changed so badly! My naivety caused me to believe and even defend her.

One time she disappeared, of course it was the day that she was supposed to get her welfare check. She gallivanted for eight days and when she came home, she had the most unbelievable story! "I was kidnapped right outside the bank, bound and put in the trunk of a car. They held me captive and then dropped me back at home, after they were finished with me." I believed it immediately, no question about it, didn't matter that it made absolutely no sense…. "Who did this to you mom?!?" I was ready to fight!

Chuck slapped me into reality *with his "Straight NO chaser" mentality*! "Shake, yo Mom is lying, she is an addict, and she left to do what addicts do! Get high and smoke up *all of their money!*" Although, I didn't want to believe it... Mom was a crackhead - the best friend I never had, was now the person I despised and loved simultaneously!

I no longer had what I wanted, and I definitely didn't have what I needed. I was left with nothing, and I was thrusted into survival mode. Quite frequently, I took toilet paper from public places, other times I raided a 'friend's' bathroom for toiletries. Sometimes, I casually walked through the store and ate whatever I wanted, then left the evidence of my "hunger-motivated" theft in the store. No, I wasn't proud of these things... I was actually quite embarrassed! I was *too afraid to 'steal' for real.*

...And then there was Eric, the man who graced my palms with at least $25 when he came to our house to see Mom. He was good to me; he knew I loved earrings and he kept me in a fresh pair of "Timbs or

Reebok Classics." Eric's lifestyle slowly but surely drew me into the drug game. I often served as a distraction for the "PoPo" during motel "transactions."

Eventually, I started cooking, bagging, and distributing cocaine… I was all about the money! I needed to survive, I had to look fly, and I had to eat - without being dependent on anyone except me [Chuck helped, but I didn't want to burden him] … because Mom was now one of the project crackheads. I knew from the time I started "my queen-pinning…" I knew these days were only temporary… it never *felt* right to me.

I felt safe doing it because Eric called me his little sister and most of the drug dealers worked for Eric. He was the "king pen" and he took care of them and made sure that they didn't do anything to disrespect me. I didn't know why I had favor until later in life, it came full circle.

Eric was my mother's 'plug'… he was the unapologetic source of my mother's disappearing acts - he fed her addiction [while she helped keep him 'in business']. His guilt (or whatever it was) made him give me $25 - $50 sporadically or supply me with a new pair of kicks because mine were worn out. I realize now, this 'money' paled in comparison to the value of my mother's life and the hundreds of thousands of dollars he made *supplying death* to other addicts. I witnessed this daily and I somehow managed to escape death...

Even though I didn't attend classes very often, I graduated high school and graduation was a big deal! My mom hadn't graduated, and I was actually the first high school graduate in my family. I was proud that my graduation was *supposed* to happen for me in Surry. The principal had given me permission to come back and 'march' with my class.

Although, I wouldn't get my diploma or anything... it was just an honorary graduation march. Chuck saved money for my bus ticket so I could get to Virginia. On the day I was supposed to leave, I couldn't find my ticket and my Mom was missing as well.

Immediately, I thought... "Mom wouldn't take my ticket, it's my 'graduation!' My exhilaration turned to a murderous hatred! How could she??? The microwave was understandable, leaving me and my sister to fend for ourselves was *doable*, but to take a moment in time from me before I could experience it... and the dream of it was still fresh in my mind, it was gone - forever! My family was waiting, my friends were anticipating, and the truth slapped all of us in the face - without warning or apology… "I am the daughter of a crackhead, and Mom had made her reality my life!"

Hopelessness consumed me in that moment, I was inconsolable, I was numb, because the only tangible connection in my life was my mother… and I felt more disconnected than I had ever felt before. I was forced to graduate with the people I barely knew in Harrisburg. I loathed everything about it!

My graduation day felt like a funeral instead of a celebration… even the damn colors were depressing. What kind of school chooses 'black and grey' for the school colors!?!?!

As fate would have it… Mom finally appeared at home the day before my graduation. When I realized she was there, I flew into attack mode! She was nothing to me in that moment *except* a "crackhead-thief-high school dropout" and the despicable definition of everything I

NEVER wanted to be! I cursed her, and she swung the first blow! It was the premiere of "Mothers & Daughters Gone Wild!" This fight wasn't cats and dogs... it was more like "lions and tigers and bears oh my!"

In the midst of our street fight, 'mommy dearest' snatched the herringbone off my neck that Chuck had given me [to assuage the pain of missing my graduation in Surry] and it fell down the tub's drain! She knew how much it meant to me, and *this* was the point I decided I no longer wanted *or needed* to be around her.

The next day, I sadly yet proudly graduated with the students of Harrisburg High... I had earned something that not even my Mom could take from me! Ironically, Carol showed up!!! The woman who stole my bus ticket, broke my chain, and beat my ass... was in the crowd yelling and screaming, "That's my baby!" like she had been "Mother of the Year" or better yet, just a mother period!

She lived up to her personal slogan of "fake it 'til you make it," during the ceremony… but I was my mother's child so I "faked it" too… "Mom who, I don't know that lady! She is crazy, probably some ole' crackhead, high on that shit!" I didn't even acknowledge her… the makeup that covered my black eye was the constant reminder that I could hide anything - even the fact that she was my biological mother!

After graduation, I 'packed' my belongings in a black trash bag and I left my mother's residence in row18 and *moved* to row 16 of the projects… I stayed with one of my Mom's friends. I had often talked with her about my life and my drug-addicted mother. She never judged me or Mom for that matter. She treated me well, I always had what I needed, no strings attached!

Her daughter called me her Big Sister and we got along fine…

One night I was downstairs sleeping on the couch, and I was awakened by the screams of the little girl. I was so afraid I remained downstairs paralyzed underneath my blanket. Then I heard footsteps walk back into another bedroom and close the door.

That happened night after night. Although, I hated leaving the little girl who called me 'Big Sister,' I didn't know what I could do. I assumed her 'stepdad' came into her room late at night and did unspeakable things that caused her scream out in fear and agony! Who would help her? Who would protect her? Why didn't her mom rescue her?

After all, these people allowed me stay there… so I dare not intrude in their business! I felt guilty. I felt like a coward… somehow, I felt as if it was my responsibility to take care of her, but I was too afraid! I couldn't even take care of myself. How could I care for someone else, a young child at that? So, I just left the whole situation

Little did I know, I had chosen to move in with Chester Molester, his girlfriend, and *their* daughter. Every night for about two weeks, I heard him creep into his four-year-old daughter's room and rape her!

Before this, Chester Molester was Mr. Cool, and I never would have believed that he was a pedophilic monster... this was too much for me. I had to *move again,* this time to the *suburbs*! Eventually he was incarcerated for molesting her, the teachers at her preschool became suspicious and the story unfolded. Meanwhile I moved in with my friend's family. I called her mom Mommy. She had been inviting me to stay with her for quite some time, I finally accepted.

When I relocated to the "hillside," with a normal family, I had chores and a curfew, I even had to ask permission to do certain things like a "normal" teenager. I respected "my new family," because they took me in… I was a complete stranger! I was "the hoodrat" and this family reminded me of "The Banks of BelAir." I did not want to disappoint them. I left my previous reality and instantly adapted to my new reality.

I had mixed emotions and the plethora of changes I survived proved I was and am a true butterfly… I may squirm initially, but I always fly in the end.

I immediately became the "Big Sister," I had two younger sisters and a baby brother. I felt welcomed, embraced, and guided *in a different way*! I was in a different world… my "new" Mommy broadened my perspectives about life, social status, religion, and relationships. I didn't worry about getting shot, mugged, or robbed *here*! There were occasional fights between teenagers that were resolved in five minutes versus the mini riots of the projects that seemingly never ended. I was living the good life, and I enrolled in a local community college.

Hillside Mommy ensured that my life was grand. She was a correctional officer and her husband worked for the state. I blended in well with the family, I shared a room with her oldest daughter, and we became best friends. We entertained typical teenage mischiefs... we went to clubs, movies, and skating. I enjoyed life with my *new* family.

Simultaneously my Hillside-Mommy was able to communicate with my biological Mom while she was at work [Carol, never knew she was talking to the person who had taken me because of her addiction and neglect.]. One day, Hillside Mommy said, "I spoke to your Mom today, you should really give her another chance, at least talk to her. She misses you! Everyone needs forgiveness and your Mom loves you despite the things she has done." I listened to Hillside Mommy, but I did not adhere to her words of wisdom.

Hillside Mommy empathized with me. She didn't dictate to me how I should feel, or even make me think I was wrong… the holistic care she provided was delicate and never judgmental. I was allotted the freedom to digest the disparity I felt. I loved and hated Carol, I wanted her but felt I was better off without her. I questioned her choice to get high rather than love me more than the "crack." Carol believed she could do both… but addiction is a delusional disease. It never allows the victim's vision to be realistic, it is always obscured!

Then one day, out of the blue, Hillside Mommy called me into her room and informed me that she was getting a divorce. We knew there was trouble in their marriage, but divorce! So, over the course of three to six months, I was told to leave and stay almost every other week. I did not resent her during this time at all, I simply needed to know I could still maintain! She had become my security, and someone I trusted with my life. I couldn't deal with *this* instability, so I prematurely married my first husband.

From the very beginning of the marriage, lies and deceit unfolded. There was one lie after another...from his age to his drug addiction! This was not the place I wanted to be. I hated him for taking advantage of my naivety and vulnerability. I also despised that I allowed him to take advantage of me because of my situation. I tried to be as comfortable as I could - being that I put myself there and always dreamt of having children.

I married him, and I assumed this was the [best] next step... but doctor after doctor told me I was not able to conceive, and I would never give birth to my own baby. The tension in the marriage escalated and lies became more frequent. I was bitter and angry... he belittled me for being "infertile." I desperately wanted to be a mother and did not give up.

Finally, I met and spoke with a doctor who gave me hope about being a mother! He informed me that if I had laparoscopic surgery, my chances of being impregnated would increase drastically. Of course, I would do anything. Surgery was a *small* price to pay. I was going to be a MOM!

On the day of the surgery my *husband* took me to the hospital, he *played* the supportive spouse role. I found out in recovery that he left shortly after I was sedated. Well, nevertheless, my morals tugged at me. He was my husband and I did want a baby…

Finally, after everything I endured… all the bad things I suffered seemingly disappeared because I was going to be a mom! I was ecstatic! Nothing could go wrong *now*, I'd come to far, been through too much…Fatefully, I received a phone call, from a woman I did not know, who cried and begged me to have an abortion. I was bewildered! Angrily perplexed, I asked "Who are you? How did you know I was pregnant? Furthermore, I don't even believe in abortion!" Then she explained, *my husband* had paid for her to get her first abortion three months ago when he found out I was pregnant… However, she was pregnant *again*!

What the hell!!! I thought this had to be a cruel joke. "Who are you?" I asked. She confessed that she had been in a sexual relationship with my husband for at least a year... basically the whole time we'd been married!

EVERYTIME he told me he had to work late or go somewhere with his job; he was *with* her! Talk about a "Love TKO!" Then she "matter-of-factly" told me what the inside of my house looked like… and verbally detailed where certain pictures were hung. I more than hated *my husband* at that moment... I called him every name in the book, and I questioned his mistress' character. What type of home-wrecking whore gets impregnated by a married man...not once but TWICE!

She sobbed incessantly as she answered every incriminating question I asked about *my husband*. She swore he told her I was his sister and she did not find out he was married until after she was pregnant the first time. Then she asserted, I am not aborting *this* pregnancy. By this time, I was like… "Blah, blah, blah bitch, you cannot rob me of my joy! I am having MY baby.

That night he came home as expected. However, when he tried to come in, I blocked the door and I told him that I had a long conversation with his *other* chick. I screamed, yelled, cursed him, and I would not allow him to enter the house. He slept on the balcony *that* night! Soon after, he disappeared, and I only saw him a few more times throughout my pregnancy.

I enjoyed every second of being pregnant... I loved the feeling of my son moving inside me. Naturally, I was consumed with questions… I had never held a baby or changed a diaper, and now I was about to be a MOM! I vowed that my baby boy would NOT go through the things I went through. Excitedly, I planned and awaited my son's BIG arrival!

Chapter 4

I Didn't Choke on the Bones...

As a "young-know-it-all," I called Dr. Jones to tell him my diagnosis and what I *needed* him to do. I was constipated and needed an emergency enema. The time was around 11pm. Since he was familiar with my personality, Dr. Jones simply agreed to meet me at the hospital, *I knew I wasn't in labor, right!*

I called my close friend at the time, for a ride to the hospital. Five minutes later, I heard a horn honk. I quickly put on my coat and went to the car. She had brought her two sisters with her. The three of them had pillows and they were excited as if they were going to a sleepover. I thought this behavior was a little strange, but I got in the car without asking for an explanation.

As we rode to the hospital, my stomach pain intensified. I thought it was due to the three grilled cheese sandwiches I had eaten earlier that day. Why did I do such a thing? I really wanted some fried fish, but everybody was too busy to get the hungry pregnant girl some food.

When we arrived at the hospital, my "friends" dropped me off at the emergency room entrance. A man dressed in medical attire, pushed a wheelchair towards me. "Who is he going to push in that thing," I thought. It was rusty, and definitely not for me!" As I slowly walked towards the entrance, I suddenly had another sharp pain shoot from my side to my lower abdomen. I kneeled to the ground, to relieve myself from the pain.

When I looked up, there was a crowd of people looking down at me. None of them asked me if they could help, but they stared as if I was a circus animal on display. The pain left as quickly as it came. I got up and screamed at the crowd, "What are you looking at!" They quickly dispersed.

I walked towards the door and that same pain struck again. This time I begged for a wheelchair, as my legs became unsteady. The hospital staff approached me with the same ugly wheelchair. I buried my pride and sat in it helplessly as I was rolled into the emergency room. They triaged me, asked my symptoms, and took my vitals. I calmly explained my awkward situation of being constipated and not being able to sleep due to the constant pressure and occasional cramping. Just as he attempted to check my blood pressure... Shannon ran into the room and screamed ecstatically, "She's in labor!!!" I politely and quite embarrassed told the nurse that my friend meant well, but she didn't know what she was talking about.

The ER nurse then asked if I was pregnant, as I was wearing regular sized clothed. "Yes, but I'm not due yet" I said sarcastically rolling my eyes. As far as I was concerned, the baby was not due until the following Friday. The man began to panic. He stuttered, "Whe whe wheennn? His facial expression and color changed right before my eyes, from nonchalant to emergent... a ghostly pale to a beet red.

He quickly raced me to the elevators as the Velcro loosened and released the BP cuff that was still on my arm. Shannon and her sisters were not far behind. As we entered the elevator, he asked them if they were coming along. They responded, "YES!" In his panicked state, he pushed the eighth floor instead of the button to open the elevator. I tried to calm him down by reassuring him I was not in labor! This was indigestion from the grilled cheese sandwiches I ate.

When we reached the eighth floor, he told the nurses I was in labor. I rudely interrupted their discussion about me, directly in front of me and explained my hysterical friends had misinformed him. Then I told them as I had told the ER attendant, my baby wasn't due until next Friday.

The nurses snickered, looked at each other and then looked at me. They said they just needed to check and make sure everything was okay. I was told to put on a pale dusty blue hospital robe. I didn't believe that I was in labor. I knew the doctor would come tell me everything was fine with my pregnancy, and he would treat my real problem, the constipation!

My "friends" walked into my room. I was irritated with them and unwelcoming to say the least. I attempted once again to convince them that, giving birth was something that would not happen that night: Reason

#1 - my water had not broken. Reason #2 - I didn't have contractions. Finally, Reason #3 - my due date was a week away!

To my relief, the doctor came in, he asked what my symptoms were and why I was at the hospital *again* (as if I hadn't told the same story already). I was upset, but I was relieved that someone listened. While I repeated my symptoms again, he checked my cervix and said, "You are already nine centimeters dilated!" I could not remember how many centimeters were necessary before labor actually began. So, I smiled and said okay, all I was sure of is that I *wasn't* in labor.

After the examination, I felt so violated that I asked to shower before I was released to go home. With a smile Dr. Jones said, "Yes, you can shower if you like… but you are not leaving tonight. You are having your son, very soon!" I was so disappointed. Dr. Jones was convinced of this rumor too. I just gave him a disapproving look and I proceeded to the shower.

As I showered, I held my sudsy body and I contemplated leaving. I was not concerned about "my friends" who drove me to the hospital, besides they were responsible for my "supposed" labor anyway.

Then... another sharp pain traveled from my abdomen to my anus, I just knew I had to "take a poop." I grunted softly. Surprisingly, the shower curtains flew open, and the nurses quickly covered my body with towels. I was laid on a "conveniently" placed gurney that wasn't there when I got in the shower and taken to the bed in "my room."

I surrendered, there wasn't one sane person in that place that would come and rescue me. The nurse and Dr. Jones poked me every few minutes. HELLO, I still felt constipated! Why weren't they helping me?

Then I heard one of them say "he has so much hair" I was convinced that everyone had lost their minds. They thought they were looking at my baby's head. How could this be? I thought I would feel some sort of pain if I was pushing an eight-pound baby out, oddly I was numb and painless. I felt nothing. I was instructed to push.

I remember hearing someone scream the head was out. Oh no, I panicked. "Oh my God! Really, my baby is coming? Now? I need pain killers!" I screamed. I wanted to make sure I had them before the pain arrived. The nurses explained to me that the hardest part was already done. I demanded something for the inevitable pending pain. They gave me a shot of Stadol. I asked for a mirror. I did not want to miss the birth of my first child. After all, I could not believe this... it was one of the most important days of my life. Nothing was going as planned; ugh I remember a tall silver mirror being rolled into the room. Shortly after, my son was on my abdomen. I had missed it.

The painkillers I just had to have made me drowsy. During that split second of childbirth I dozed off and missed the beautiful miracle of life. But as I held my baby boy, I was overwhelmed with emotion. I marinated in my new reality of motherhood! I knew my life would never be the same.

I realized there was so much I didn't know. I was speechless. I did not know how to care for this little innocent child. My "I's" would become "we," I had to change my mentality from selfishness to selflessness... Was I even ready? Was I capable of being a "good" mother?

It was ironic that during the pregnancy, I believed I had all the answers. I thought everything would go as I planned. Because of my "know it all-ness" I experienced my first labor, and yet I completely missed the birth of my son. I sobbed softly as I looked into his big brown eyes. I wanted... better yet I needed to make him proud, to be a good mom, and keep him safe. I quickly switched gears. I had a new priority.

Chapter 5

Mission Unaccomplished

Cooked, cleaned, and had my babies... now what?

Motherhood is multifaceted; it is complicated and extremely difficult to articulate. What does it mean to be a good mother? How do you know *if* you're a good mother? Who determines or more importantly, what defines 'a good mother?'

In all honesty, being a mother caused me to see things from several different perspectives. Motherhood has caused me to be less critical. I've learned each child has a different personality and behaviors which a mother must adapt to, so she can effectively parent them as an individual; while considering their unique gifts, talents, and even their shortcomings.

Understanding a child's individuality, causes a mother to respond in a variety of different ways to the same exact situation. I've learned that unless we know the entire story or have walked in *that* mother's shoes or in the shoes of the child… we do not have the right to comment on the parenting style or the behavior of the child.

Some people are innate nurturers… but being a mother, is a combination of trial and error, instincts, and even genetics play a part in this thing we know as mothering. Motherhood changes, and the type of mother she will be is directly connected to that mother's stage of her life. Giving birth made me a mother biologically… but the infinite influences internally and externally made mothering a lifestyle.

Life is never the same after entering this realm. Not one child comes with instructions. Thus, motherhood is complex, there is no simplicity. It is not black, white, or even gray… but motherhood is a myriad of colorful experiences. As a mother I love each of my children differently but undeniably equal.

I have come to the realization that I had to learn how to be a mother to each of my children; what works for one child, may not work for the other. The depth of motherhood is something that is instinctive, it simultaneously occurs and changes as we change, and as our children change.

Does motherhood define me? Yes, it does… but only partially. Has it caused me to evolve into a different person than I was before my reality of parenting? Absolutely. Am I the definition of motherhood, for my children? Slightly. I say this because I believe in teaching independence and preparation to deal with the world. So, I'm always planning and preparing for the future and therefore I prepare my children to make decision regarding their future, solidify their plan, and even have backup plans (options are always necessary). The best way I know how to define motherhood, is to always be prepared and ready, we cannot control what's coming but we can control our response!

Big Momma's teaching caused me to think that getting married and having babies *should be* my ultimate goal in life. However, I realized my life exceeded mothering, because my children *will* exceed or dismiss my expectations of them. I am certain, that I am the manifested dreams of my mother(s). Fortunately, I also strive to be all the things I believe are beneficial for my life. Consequently, each time I arrived at a "what now," moment in my life... I strived towards the greatness of a new goal, because my mission is unaccomplished!

Chapter 6

I Am My Mothers' Child

I am my mother's child… but which mother?

Well, I am a combination of all three of my mothers. My

choices and decisions are based on the powerful women

that influenced my life.

I am *Carol* [my biological mother aka Mom]. I am

a survivor, a chameleon of sorts. I am a free-spirit; I

embrace life for what it is and what it is worth at the

time and seek new adventures. I am *Carol*, quick witted

and sarcastic. I live to make my ancestors proud of me.

My Mom was my biggest cheerleader and my best friend.

No one has or will ever compare to the bond we shared.

I learned from *my Mom's* mistakes. Her vivid and

candid tendency with me about everything intrigued me

and pushed me to realms that I did not believe I could

reach. Ironically, by NOT being an "example/role

model" according to society's standards, *Carol* taught me *what to do by showing me what I NEVER wanted to do.*

And yes, I am *also* Big Momma - absolutely! My values and morals were instilled by her... to this day I have never smoked a cigarette. I've never gotten high. "I have never'd" quite a few things, not because I can't or couldn't, but because of the self-respect she ingrained within me. I'm methodical, I plan and consider all other options and/or obstacles that may interfere with my plan(s).

I remain ready at all times, and I always have a backup just in case. I am traditional and sentimental. I truly value relationships, I am innately nurturing and loyal. Big Momma taught me that rules aren't always for me... some rules are meant to be broken! Sometimes it is necessary to test the limits, not accept barriers, and push myself beyond societal or personal expectations. I embrace my dreams and aspire to exceed life's limitations.

I am also Mommy. I religiously practice unorthodox thinking. I explore revelations of life. I am analytical and spiritual. I am aware of my history, my culture, social injustices and conspiracies. Mommy, teaches me to think for myself, trust myself, and believe in myself despite what other people *may* believe.

It is because of her that the latest fads don't phase me. Other people's opinions of me are not my problem, and she taught me self-love, no regrets... just lessons learned. Because of her, I boldly embrace who I am and who I am becoming; without dismissing where I've come from.

The sacrifices of my ancestors will never be forgotten because of *"Mommy's Skooling."* She taught me to be determined, and to be confident that I can do whatever I want to do... I just have to figure out how

and then make it happen at the right time! I am

motivated because I realize, chance happens to everyone,

and being ready is the key to seizing irreplaceable

chances!

Chapter 7

Evolving Transitions

...Becoming Better!

My Mom did eventually get clean. She gained my trust and once again entered my life, but this time not only was she mom, but Grandma too. She was so proud to be a Grandma. Issaiah was a precious trophy to her. Everything he did was incredibly cute. He had the same birthmark as she did in her eye. They were a pair to say the least.

I enjoyed this 'clean' Mom and was happy to have my bestie back. She was so resourceful and gave amazing advice on pacifying a teething baby, how to calm a baby to sleep through the night, how to break a fever, and soothe a cough. Mom was the best grandma ever to my son and she spent time with him regularly. She took him more often and to more places than she did her other grandchildren. I felt that she and Issaiah had a special bond.

Mom was still Mom, she did not watch him when I wanted or needed her to, but whenever she felt like it. She was so unpredictable. She often let me drop him off or come and pick him up and she took him to the park, playground, and sometimes the fair... whatever was going on, there was no such thing as "no" with Grandma Carol! Issaiah was all smiles with Grandma. They had a connection that was unbreakable. At times I wished I had *had* that experience with Carol.

Fortunately, Issaiah only knew her as a loving, caring, clean, and fun Grandma. This was her attempt to try and rectify the things she failed to do with me. Although, their time together was brief, she made every second worth it! My heart was and is extremely grateful for that.

Mom's Eternal Transition

I was awakened from my sleep right before sunrise, I rolled over and tried to ignore the banging on my door! Unfortunately, whoever was there was annoyingly persistent. I became an infuriated beast! "Damn Jehovah's Witnesses," I thought as I stomped my way downstairs to give them a piece of my mind! I opened the door and saw it was my Mom's neighbor. She came in and told me my Mom was in the hospital. I wanted to say, "You could have called me for that, instead of waking me up..." but I didn't. I uttered "Okay," and I tried to keep a straight face and not reveal my irritation. "I'll see her once I get Issaiah up and fed." Ms. Neighbor said, "No you need to go now!" I wasn't in a rush because the entire situation seemed so strange. If there was a true emergency - Ms. Neighbor would not have been my informant. Why her??? I was beyond confused and aggravated.

For several moments (or minutes) we exchanged unnecessary conversation… I finally thought "Why are you bullshitting me!" Then Ms. Neighbor blurted out "Your Mom died!" What the hell, is this a cruel joke? What in the world is going on here! I screamed, "Well, why did you start out telling me she was just in the hospital? You want me to go there and see a dead person!" I was furious… and I told her to leave.

Immediately, my great aunt called me revealing the same shocking news but explaining that due to the fact that I was the eldest among my siblings, it was my responsibility to identify the body. In that moment, I wished somebody would have told me of my mother's demise to start with… I had so many questions!!!! What happened? I just talked to Mom yesterday.

Nevertheless, I got in my car and went to the hospital but when I got there it was too late - I couldn't say goodbye, or I love you one last time. Sadly, this possibility was ripped from my grasp due to *Ms. Neighbor's* ignorance. My sister identified the body prior to my arrival. I watched in saddened disbelief as the coroner drove away from the hospital. I had missed it. I was angry … and I was consumed with unexplainable guilt. I was perplexed. More than anything I was not ready for Mom's passing.

Our (me and mom's) relationship had finally reached a point of genuine admiration… and now she was gone *forever*! She was my rock, but more importantly Mom was the rock for my son! I had no idea how to move forward… however, I knew I couldn't just stand still…but death is the only entity that has the ability to stop everything - even the things that are *still* living.

So, I went home and packed...I did the only thing I could think of. I drove to New York - my mother's home. I went to Brooklyn. I went to Manhattan. Then I went along Coney Island. I don't know what I was looking for or what I wanted to feel. I simply wanted to be where my Mom was rooted, where she was sincerely happy.

Mom's death devastated me to my core. The finality of it was almost too much for me to bear. Death doesn't allow "do-overs" only start-overs. I didn't have a chance to say my 'last' goodbye - eternity didn't wait for me. I was left with the guilt, the shame, and the antagonizing desire for one more chance.

I became angry at God, and at times angry at her! Heartbroken, I was left with the responsibility of arranging everything regarding her funeral – from choosing the funeral home to writing her obituary. All because I was the eldest, I somehow inherited this inescapable task.

My Life after Mom's Death

Mom's death left me hollow, scared, and lonely. I feel as if part of me died. I wavered between being confident and proud because I felt as I was left in a world that did not understand me. I felt insignificant, nameless, like a number in line of endless people… a statistic of sorts! Yes, Mom's death changed me. I wrestled often with the grief to keep it from robbing me of my ambition, my optimism, and my belief in all that is 'good.'

I became stagnant for first year and as soon as I finally attempted to move on… I received Mom's autopsy report. It was like a punch in the neck that shoved me backwards down the stairwell of life and it halted my healing process. It has been several years, and as I pick up the scattered pieces and try to progress forward. I realize I was birthed to an angel that had to return sooner than I wanted or expected. My Mom taught me how to love hard, make selfless decisions, put my children's needs before my own, and to NEVER stop trying to become better, do better, and be better... Therefore, I will always be in a state of evolution.

About the Author

Amelia Starr Isom is much more than what meets your eyes when you *just see* her. Unsurprisingly, her appearance is quite beguiling, and her beautifully demure exterior has probably saved her from situations, people, and experiences that could have been detrimental.

Amelia is a wife, mother, health professional, entrepreneur, and *now* a published author! Her life is a testament to the adage, "Life is a concoction of tribulation and triumph, but if you get up more times than you fall… YOU will *always* be triumphant!" Although, life takes us by surprise, it doesn't have to shock us into the pits of despair.

Amelia incessantly strives to be the best version of who she is destined to be! Unapologetically, she lives a fulfilling and happy life. With a name like Starr, she is destined to illuminate the world!

CPSIA information can be obtained
at www.ICGtesting.com
Printed in the USA
FSHW020328261020
75197FS